One Minute

with

for WOMEN

HOPE LYDA

HARVEST HOUSE PUBLISHERS

EUGENE, OREGON

Cover by Garborg Design Works, Savage, Minnesota

ONE MINUTE WITH GOD FOR WOMEN
Copyright © 2008 by Hope Lyda
Published by Harvest House Publishers
Eugene, Oregon 97402
www.harvesthousepublishers.com

ISBN-13: 978-0-7369-2167-1
ISBN-10: 0-7369-2167-2

Printed in the United States of America

08 09 10 11 12 13 14 15 16 / BP-NI / 10 9 8 7 6 5 4 3 2 1

Contents

Introduction 5

Transformation 7

Renewal 21

Patience and Peace 35

Abundance 49

Contentment 63

Intentional Living 77

Dreams and Aspirations 91

Hope 105

Wholeness 119

Discovery 133

Just a Minute…

One minute? That's what you allot an egg to be cooked for breakfast, a commercial to entice you, a meter to keep you ticket free for a quick stop. So one minute with God seems a bit…meager. Ah, but a minute can turn into so much more.

You're busy. You probably send up prayers throughout the day asking for a second pair of hands, patience in the bank line, and energy for a task. But when you turn your focus to God for a minute, your heart opens up to his hope for your future and his vision for your life.

May these brief devotions and prayers become the breathing space you long for during your busiest days. God's presence is a sanctuary you'll want to return to more and more as one minute transforms into a lifetime of connection with your Creator.

Transformation

Words of Transformation

The way to become wise is to honor the LORD;
he gives sound judgment to all
who obey his commands.

PSALM 111:10 TEV

⌐⌐⌐

Jesus called a child to come and stand in front
of them, and said, "I assure you that unless
you change and become like children, you
will never enter the Kingdom of heaven."

MATTHEW 18:2-3 TEV

⌐⌐⌐

Some, however, did receive him and believed
in him; so he gave them the right to become
God's children. They did not become
God's children by natural means, that is,
by being born as the children of a human
father; God himself was their Father.

JOHN 1:12-13 TEV

What is mortal must be changed into
what is immortal; what will die must
be changed into what cannot die.

1 CORINTHIANS 15:53 TEV

Keep your roots deep in him, build your lives on him, and become stronger in your faith, as you were taught. And be filled with thanksgiving.

Colossians 2:7 tev

~~~

All things are done according to God's plan and decision; and God chose us to be his own people in union with Christ because of his own purpose, based on what he had decided from the very beginning. Let us, then, who were the first to hope in Christ, praise God's glory!

Ephesians 1:11-12 tev

~~~

Perseverance must finish its work so that you may be mature and complete, not lacking anything.

James 1:4

New Attitude

My friend is trying new things. New healthy habits. New ways of approaching her fears. New attitudes. These changes don't feel awkward to her; they feel familiar, comfortable, a perfect fit. Funny how it takes change, small and big, internal and external, for you to become more like yourself—to fit the heart and purpose God gave you from the very beginning.

If you set out to "find yourself," you're headed for a long road with many twists and intersections. And an elusive destination. But when you embark on a journey to find who you are in God, the destination is unwavering. You'll feel more like your true self with each step you take.

I want to find the way to the fulfilling life you have planned for me, God. With each change or decision that I turn over to your guidance, I know I will come closer to the "me" you created.

Change of Path

Our brains create routes to memories, emotions, ideas, and responses. These serve us well, unless those embedded routes lead us to crumbled roads of routine anger, depression, and self-deception. When we embrace faith, God's grace renews our minds and hearts; we're no longer stuck in or imprisoned by old behaviors and thoughts.

Have you experienced this infusion of hope and transformation? It might take time for your broken thinking and broken living to be replaced by God's truth and peace. But your prayers for new patterns are heard. And new ways are being shaped in you. Trust the changes that usher you toward a whole faith.

God, create new ways for me to approach life, hope, and my future. When my past hurts lead to broken thinking, renew my thoughts. Fill my mind with the hope of faith and the peace of a transformed heart.

Finding Your Voice

Do you know what you sound like? Beyond the voice you use to ask for help around the house or to request a memo at work. What do you say to yourself when silence surrounds you and thoughts start swirling? These are often the moments when your true voice emerges. It reminds you of your faith, your value, your gifts, and your dreams. And God knows that voice—he hears it when you pray, when you struggle, when you silently call out for help, when you lift up a secret hope.

A woman's life is transformed when she rediscovers the voice God gives her. Allow time to hear it and to treasure it.

You know the sound my heart makes when it calls out to you. You've heard my tears fall and seen my hopes rise. Lead me to know my voice and to use it to proclaim your goodness.

The Redemption of Flaws

What about your behavior gets old—even to you? I'll start with a few from my list of sometimes-annoying attributes: shyness, sarcasm, indecisiveness, messiness...When left unpolished and jagged, these behaviors work against my purpose. But when given over to God's grace, they're like the bit of sand wedged in an oyster's home...transformed over time and effort into a pearl. My indecisiveness will never be lovely, but the transformed version will be.

What does your spouse or friend or coworker do that rubs you the wrong way? Give those, too, to God; let irritation lead to transformation in you and in your relationships.'

There's so much I do that can drive me nuts.
I'm sorry for the times when my example is such
a shallow representation of your holiness. May
I turn over to you each of my less-than-lovely
characteristics so that I can become more like you.

Ongoing Education

Did you miss class this week? God's class is always going on. And there were quite a few lessons to be learned in the past few days. How much of your faith education do you miss because you aren't aware, taking notes, or showing up for your life?

In a very miraculous way, God is always bringing teachers to our paths. We'll learn new ways to hope and help, and skills to grow in faith and compassion. We never finish discovering more about how life and faith intersect, how God loves, and how we're to love others. In fact, when we naively say "I've arrived!" a big life lesson is about to hit!

Let me watch for the teachers you bring into my life. I'm so thankful for those who reach out to me when I need connection, those who express your wisdom when I struggle, and those who stand firm when I'm floundering. Help me to glean truth from these examples.

Between Here and There

Travels to a foreign land or a nearby town or a rarely visited forest offer opportunities to depend on God in new ways. I've been places where I didn't know the language and had to rely on God's leading to make the journey safely. He'd reroute me with a tug of intuition when I'd wander. He'd present the person or form of transportation I needed.

Each time I travel, God gives me the vision to see his interaction with me on a very personal level. I never feel closer to him than when I'm totally dependent. Even if you don't have plane tickets tucked away for an upcoming adventure, rely on God for your daily needs, direction, shelter, connections with people, etc. The gift of travel graces is a part of your everyday life.

Help me to depend on you for everything, God. When I feel like I know what to expect, I start to rely on my strength rather than your power. I truly am a visitor journeying through this life. I need to act like it!

The Unfolding of a Life

Life's always changing around us. Friends take new jobs, move across the country, start families, get divorced, watch kids leave, discover their passions, come to faith, question God, and on and on. Do you feel such shifts happening in your own life? Or do you resist change as much as possible because you don't want to disturb your sense of security?

When each day looks the same, when your calendar for this year matches that of last year, when your wish list, group of friends, or menu of struggles and grudges is exactly the same, it's time for change. I know change is hard. But by fearfully avoiding potentially bad stuff, you've avoided the good stuff. Allow your life to unfold.

I'm ready to view change as a good thing. I've fought transitions in the past because they made me feel alone and out of control. I tried to control the outcome rather than turn it over to you. This change I'm facing...I'll see it as an opportunity.

Take Your Own Advice

"Just be yourself!" We speak this affirmation with fervent enthusiasm to others who are feeling left out because of their uniqueness or perceived weaknesses. We champion the underdog with the phrase because something about it resounds with truth in our hearts. We believe it. We do. But do we believe it in a big way for our own lives?

We'll go to great lengths to be like others, to become special editions of ourselves (only the ideal parts), or to present airbrushed versions (only the fake, ideal parts). When will we love who we are? Yes, we can improve. Yes, we'll still experience transformation. But we are to be ourselves—*this* is what makes faith and life work. "Just be yourself" is a call to know yourself as God does.

When will I accept the me you know and love? I've tried to pursue paths that were not mine to pursue. I've longed for dreams that weren't mine to entertain. And I've pushed myself to be something I'm not. It feels good to be back here as myself. As your child.

Let It Rise

What potential is forming in your heart and spirit that needs nurturing? You think of it when you're standing in line, wiping the counter, folding laundry, typing an email. It breaks into your thoughts with a flash and disappears into the mundane. But this elusive idea longs to be given weight and dimension, and the time it takes to gain such importance.

Let what is becoming rise up in you. Give it attention, a quiet place to rest, and encouragement when it is ready to take shape. Don't brush aside these pieces of yourself. God leads you to truths that are waiting to rise up and become parts of your life.

I'm rarely silent enough to hear your still small voice. But when I focus, close my mouth, and open my heart, I sense your leading. I'm amazed when I get a glimpse of the dream you're shaping in me, God.

Which Way?

I ask God for a clearer sign to identify where I'm at and where I might be headed. If I'm on the road less traveled, I question why more people haven't thought to go this route if it is of such value. When I'm rushing alongside the masses on the highway of success, ambition, or status quo, then I wonder why more people don't think to leave this chaos.

Which road are you on? Do you look around at your home, your family, and your job and wonder if you are on God's intended path? Rest in today. Rest in the choices you've made that have directed you here. Do not give God your "what ifs" as an offering; instead, give him your commitment to go forward with faith and peace.

Which way, God? Others around me are choosing
paths, some with certainty and some with timidity.
I want to experience the peace of moving forward.
I know that when I trust you and rest in your
faithfulness, I can walk with sure steps.

Renewal

Words of Renewal

He put a new song in my mouth,
a hymn of praise to our God.
Many will see and fear
and put their trust in the LORD.

PSALM 40:3

Create in me a pure heart, O God,
and renew a steadfast spirit within me.

PSALM 51:10

My soul finds rest in God alone;
my salvation comes from him.
He alone is my rock and my salvation;
he is my fortress, I will never be shaken.

PSALM 62:1-2

A generous man will prosper;
he who refreshes others will himself be refreshed.

PROVERBS 11:25

Even youths grow tired and weary,
and young men stumble and fall;
but those who hope in the LORD
will renew their strength.

ISAIAH 40:30-31

Forget the former things;
do not dwell on the past.
See, I am doing a new thing!
Now it springs up; do you not perceive it?
I am making a way in the desert
and streams in the wasteland.

ISAIAH 43:18-19

You were wearied by all your ways,
but you would not say, "It is hopeless."
You found renewal of your strength,
and so you did not faint.

ISAIAH 57:10

I will give you a new heart and put a new
spirit in you; I will remove from you your
heart of stone and give you a heart of flesh.

EZEKIEL 36:26

Real Freedom

Are you eager to have an exuberant, joyful faith? Do you want a faith that soars high above mediocrity? First, you might have to cut some ties that keep your growth and belief confined to worldly standards. There is someone you know (quite well, actually) who might be restricting you with limited power, understanding, and wisdom.

Okay, it's you! If you're relying on yourself to gain the freedom and joy of the Lord, you've probably gone as far as you can go. Get out from under your own control! And experience the real freedom of faith.

My own power is so limited. So is my wisdom and understanding. Why do I still think I should be in charge of my life? God, help me to release my grip on my days, my purpose, my future so that the real freedom of living in your strength becomes mine.

On a Limb

When you're used to clinging to things of the world to ground you, secure you to meaning, the life of belief can be scary! It can also be exhilarating. Even if you clung to the tree for a long time before stepping out on the limb of belief, you're an adventuress! You're learning to rely on God's strength and security with every step. And he faithfully takes you forward and shows you the vista of purpose from up on high.

Close your eyes, feel the breeze on your face, and reach out for God's leading. Experience the delight of this new kind of living.

There's much left for me to see, discover, learn, and celebrate! Each time I seek your will and strive to live abundantly, I am an adventuress. It's amazing to consider the heights to which you will take me and to know that the horizon ahead is one you created for me.

Bright Eyed

It's fun to watch the faces of people holding a baby. They stretch their smiles, purse their lips, and lift their eyebrows. They mirror what they're watching in the face of the infant. In that moment when bright eyes meet wide eyes, there's an uplifting of heart and soul.

If our journeys are reflecting the countenance of God, there'll be many moments of bright eyes and hopeful smiles. This day, this moment, is a part of God's amazing, miraculous creation. Mirror his delight in the gift of living!

God, do I reflect you in my life? Is there an expression I make or a gesture I extend that reflects your image? I want to show you to others, and I want to show you the joy of my faith.

Spiritual Makeover

Is your spiritual life sagging? Is a once-active faith now a matter of "doing the right thing"? As women, we give a lot to others. Even when this is done with willing, servants' hearts, it can cause us to ignore our living faith. If your belief system is more system than belief, it's time for a spiritual makeover.

Determine what's missing from your life with God. Maybe it's been years since you totally depended on him. Maybe you haven't prayed from a place of absolute need and hope. Walk into the presence of God. Ask for renewal of spirit, mind, body, and soul. Rejuvenate your faith.

God, more than I need to be right,
or perceived as perfect...I need you. I know that
the life of faith isn't about perfection. I want
to free myself from the expectations of others so
that I can live fully under the covering of your
hope and grace. Show me what's missing.

Refinish

If you've ever taken on the project of turning a drab piece of forgotten furniture into a showcase item for your home, you know how much work is involved in making something new again...or better than new. First you must strip away the build-up of finish and stains—long forgotten versions of what is aesthetic. Then you see that hint of newness and natural beauty; the result is a treasure.

Do other people's versions of beauty, worthiness, and value still cover your life? Do stains of sin and loss and pain dull your heart? With God's grace, you can remove those layers. It might take work, tears, and times of questioning, but the life that emerges will be the one God wants to see shine. It will be a treasure.

God, please strip away my layers of sin, mistakes, arrogance, stubbornness, and rebellion. They've obscured my purpose and beauty. When I try to do the right thing, it's often with selfish motives. I want the treasure of my faith and heart to be revealed.

Open to Be Filled

Why is it that when I have work to do that requires an attentive mind, all I want to do is paint a room or rearrange my bookshelf? Organizing my hall closet suddenly seems like the perfect afternoon activity. This frustrates me until I realize that I'm hungering for what I need. These activities feed me, fuel me, and allow me to settle once again into more focused work.

So it goes with the faith life. If you spend all your time analyzing how God works, contemplating the origin of the universe, and scrutinizing your commitment to faith, God is probably nudging you to take a breath, plant a flower, write a note, organize a kitchen cupboard, and allow yourself to be emptied so that you can then be filled with him.

Okay, it's hard for me to let go of some things. I'll think a question or concern to death and then wonder why I don't feel peace. Help me to see the world of beauty around me. May I be inspired to savor life and feel a renewal of my spirit.

Step Aside

The day can become all about what you say, what you do, where you put your car keys, the time you wasted looking for your car keys. But when you pause and consider life beyond you, you'll discover what God wants you to notice.

There are times when God asks you to live beyond your needs and the thoughts rolling about in your mind so that you can listen to others, meet their needs, hear their opinions, and learn about their journeys. Step aside for the day; be God's ears, eyes, and hands.

If I'd just look up from my to-do list and stop checking for voice mails, I'd notice the things you have for me to do. They aren't always a part of my human agenda. Who should I meet? What long-forgotten dream should I resurrect? Show me.

Useful

I decided to start composting this year. People who do it right end up with wonderful nourishment for their flowers, shrubs, and vegetables. I love it because my broken broccoli stems, wilted lettuce, and eggshells no longer stink up my kitchen's 13-gallon wastebasket. Instead, this leftovers cocktail will become useful material.

God, the Master Gardener, does a lot of composting in our lives. When we give him our debris—our wilted spirits, the shells of our egos, the broken pieces of our lives—he tends to them. He turns our losses and our sins into the useful material of faith.

My past mistakes are useless. They pile up and start to decay. Yet I walk around carrying them like it makes sense. I'm crazy. You're not only willing, but longing to take this debris from me and exchange it for beauty, direction, and peace. Please make my brokenness and wasted moments useful.

Starting Over

Some friends are dealing with divorce and its aftermath. Others are at the crossroads of choosing a new job or even a new profession. Moms face empty homes as grown children reach for their futures. Life is filled with transitions—some we hope for, some we avoid as long as possible. Give yourself over to the chance to start over!

There's so much to discover about yourself and God when you face transitions with your heart open to what the next opportunity has to offer. Sadly, many of us wait until *major* transitions take place before we trust in God's leading. Each choice, each dream, each hope, and each heartache can be given over to God's capable hands.

Show me how to handle this transition with grace.
I'm a bit scared, and I certainly have a lot of doubt.
But you're ready to lead me. You take my shaky hand
and guide me through what seems like an ending
but becomes a beginning. A beautiful beginning.

Breaktime

It's good to get away from the pressures of life. How often do you take a nap? a vacation? a bubble bath? It's breaktime—starting now. What will you do with it? What do you long for? What has God been placing on your heart—you know, the dream you ignore time after time?

When's the last time you gave yourself a break? Do you count up your indiscretions at the end of the day? Do you beat yourself up every time you slip and fall? There's a lot of living to be done on the other side of self-loathing. Give yourself a break, and discover the peace God offers.

As a kid, I'd wake from a nap with an eagerness for whatever came next. If I'd had a bad morning, I could easily start over after a good rest. As an adult, I need a break from my angst, my worries, and my self-reprimands so that I can eagerly receive your grace and your fresh plans for my life.

Patience
and Peace

Words of Patience and Peace

I know, my God, that you test the heart
and are pleased with integrity.

1 Chronicles 29:17

⟡

Submit to God and be at peace with him;
in this way prosperity will come to you.
Accept instruction from his mouth
and lay up his words in your heart.

Job 22:21-22

⟡

The Lord gives strength to his people;
the Lord blesses his people with peace.

Psalm 29:11

⟡

Seek peace and pursue it.

Psalm 34:14

⟡

Consider the blameless, observe the upright;
there is a future for the man of peace.

Psalm 37:37

I wait for you, O Lord;
you will answer, O Lord my God.

Psalm 38:15

～～～

You will keep in perfect peace
him whose mind is steadfast,
because he trusts in you.

Isaiah 26:3

～～～

[Jesus] got up, rebuked the wind and said
to the waves, "Quiet! Be still!" Then the
wind died down and it was completely
calm. He said to his disciples, "Why are you
so afraid? Do you still have no faith?"

Mark 4:39-40

～～～

We do not want you to become lazy, but to
be like those who believe and are patient,
and so receive what God has promised.

Hebrews 6:12 tev

Silence Is Golden

Light a candle. Draw the blinds. Turn off the television. Take a seat. Introduce yourself to silence. It can be uncomfortable at first. Even later on. But without it, your heart has no space to find God. The noises that create a constant soundtrack to your life need to be quieted once in awhile.

In the silence, your long-neglected worries, praises, hopes, and truths will rise up and be offered to the Lord. Don't drown out these heartfelt prayers.

*Resting in your peace eases my soul. The endless
questions and doubts stop midflight. My shoulders
relax; they no longer have to bear all the burdens
of my world. My heart calms; it no longer
has to keep up with my unrealistic pace.*

The Big Break

I know it'll happen any day now—the big break that will take my life to the next level of happiness, hope, and potential. Do you feel that too? Are you waiting for your big break? A sudden flood of cash, a career boost, a knight in shining armor, a launch to fame, the perfect alignment of time and money so that you can finally accomplish your dream?

Sometimes waiting is the practice of godly patience. Sometimes it is purely an act of futility—a deferment of living. Don't you know…while we're waiting for our respective big breaks, God is waiting for a break in our holding pattern? He's hoping we'll recognize the happiness, hope, and potential in the day we're living, the relationship we are in, and the dream we're walking toward.

When I'm waiting futilely for worldly success or recognition or an open door that has long been shut, help me to move on. Give me words of wisdom through others and through my time in prayer. I want to recognize my big break…my chance to live the big life of faith.

Waiting for What's There

Have you ever waited for a friend to call or make a move to show her loyalty? When you're feeling lonely, thoughts can shift to how others aren't available or attentive enough. You'll look for faults in others to find the reason for your own sadness. When night comes and you've been waiting all day for assurance, God's grace is here to cover you, his love is here to fill that void.

While you're looking for someone to blame or someone to save you from loneliness, God is with you. He is waiting for you to call on him.

I used to try and ignore the loneliness I'd feel from time to time. Or I'd pretend it related to how someone else was treating me or acting toward me. The truth is, my loneliness is often an ache for intimacy with you. Your love is meant to fill me.

Clarity

Anger and frustration rise up in me and take me by surprise. I'm short with strangers and curt with loved ones. I feel the need to get clarity. I've lost perspective. I need distance to witness what my behavior is and to keep it in check.

Does your attitude or lack of reason ever shock you? Let God be your outside perspective. He provides wake-up calls so that we get a glimpse of what he sees happening. His peace can calm our anger. His compassion can make us tender again. His grace allows us to speak with love. His perspective gives us the clarity we need to turn to him for help.

I don't always hear myself or see my actions clearly until I do something that is blatantly unkind. God, when I'm feeling edgy or irritated, help me bring my troubles to you. Help me search my heart for the source of the hurt, the indifference, or the anger.

A New Emphasis

It's difficult to notice the blessings in your life when all you see are the demands, expectations, responsibilities, and daily grind. Was there an actual point of exchange when you traded living for talking about, shopping for, plotting out, and managing a life?

Are you in this spot? There's a surprisingly simple remedy: Change the emphasis. Allow each day to be about living, not the strings attached that make it go. Give those to God. View your planner as a friend rather than a ruler. It's difficult to notice the demands, expectations, and responsibilities when all you see are the blessings.

No more just managing my life. I want to live it! My life's path is often all about what society demands of me. I want to hunger only for your requests of my time, heart, energy, talents, and soul. May I seek out your calling, and may I honor the blessings you provide.

Peace March

What do you stand for? Do your words express bitterness or forgiveness? Do you present the case for mercy or judgment? Do you extend hostility or hospitality? Do you side with the powerful or champion the weak? Do you remain silent, or do you speak out against injustice? Do you correct, or do you encourage? Do you hoard, or do you give? Do you expect, or do you offer? Do you pick apart others, or do you piece them together?

Are you willing to be a reflection of Christ? Move forward in faith. Start walking toward a life that stands for something.

My heart needs to be softened, Lord. I become jaded too easily. I want my daily actions and words to reflect a spirit of peace, compassion, and tenderness. I long to stand for your goodness by showing unconditional love and endless mercy.

My Blankie!

Hand it over. I know you have one—an adult version of a blankie. No? Take a look at what you reach for every time you need a sense of security. When things spin out of control, what comforts you? There are many security blankets that clutter our existence, even as rational adults—food, work, sex, television, computer games, emails, material possessions, shopping for those possessions, lashing out at others, and so on.

Our temporal options feel good initially, but as is the nature of things of the world…they become tattered, ineffective substitutions for God's peace. When you need assurance, comfort, and an anchor to purpose, reach for the blanket of God's grace and security.

I don't wanna let go! This security blanket has seen me through trials in my work and my relationships. It was with me when I had an identity crisis. But I know it's time to relinquish my hold…it will never be a substitute for my assurance in and of you.

Small Talk

I talk to God about the hidden part of my soul, the darkest corner of my fear, and the brightest spark of my hope. But now and then I'll start with small talk, like we've just met. I'll stammer a bit, discuss the weather, or what I'm going to do tomorrow. Then God gives me his peace. He reassures me that anything I say is important to him.

And just like that, I move from shallow conversation to the deep waters of soulful prayer. I can barely contain myself, because I want him to know all of me, and I want to know all of him. Are you caught in a cycle of small talk? God is with you, and he's nodding, smiling, and waiting—not to be entertained by you—but to be trusted and known.

God, I'm here with the good and the bad. I want to get personal and real and intimate with you. You picked the colors of my soul. You know me when I am scared to know myself. Are you ready for the deep end of my prayers?

What I Mean Is...

Are you frequently explaining yourself and your ideas over and over to the same people? It can be frustrating when you feel like nobody gets you and what you're about. Our desire to be heard and understood is our hunger for significance in this lifetime.

You are significant. You are heard. And you are seen completely by your Creator. Your hunger is very real, and it is also a blessing. It will draw you to God. It will lead you to seek fulfillment and identity in his grace.

God, it's a great security and comfort to speak to you from my heart and be heard. You don't dismiss me. You don't see my struggles as minor even though they don't compare with those of many of your children. What I mean is...thank you for loving me.

Today Is Sacred

You can go on a pilgrimage to a far-off land to understand the sacred. You can practice traditions that honor what is holy. But the sacred is even more accessible. You can experience it through daily living. We make the pursuit of holiness too complicated. We introduce conflict and drama where there's supposed to be simplicity and peace.

Your life is sacred. There's nothing ordinary or trivial about who you are and what you do. Center your life in God's peace, and live with full awareness of God's love. When you celebrate the privilege of being alive and knowing God, you're savoring the sacred.

I've traveled far emotionally. This journey of trial and doubt was not required by you, yet somehow it felt necessary for my own understanding of faith. Help me to hold on to your love wherever I am. I wish to carry the sacred with me from this point onward.

Abundance

Words of Abundance

Let my teaching fall like rain
and my words descend like dew,
like showers on new grass,
like abundant rain on tender plants.

DEUTERONOMY 32:2

You anoint my head with oil;
my cup overflows. Surely goodness and love
will follow me all the days of my life,
and I will dwell in the house of the LORD forever.

PSALM 23:5-6

They will tell of the power of your awesome
works, and I will proclaim your great deeds.
They will celebrate your abundant goodness
and joyfully sing of your righteousness.

PSALM 145:6-7

He will also send you rain for the seed you
sow in the ground, and the food that comes
from the land will be rich and plentiful.

ISAIAH 30:23

I will bring health and healing to [this city];
I will heal my people and will let them
enjoy abundant peace and security.

JEREMIAH 33:6

~

You will have plenty to eat, until you are full,
and you will praise the name
of the LORD your God,
who has worked wonders for you;
never again will my people be shamed.

JOEL 2:26

~

From the fullness of his grace we have all
received one blessing after another.

JOHN 1:16

~

In union with Christ you have become rich in all
things, including all speech and all knowledge.

1 CORINTHIANS 1:5 TEV

~

God did not give us a spirit of timidity, but a
spirit of power, of love and of self-discipline.

2 TIMOTHY 1:7

Affluence or Influence

I don't know which income-level box you check on your tax forms. I don't know if you own a vacation home or rent a one-bedroom apartment. But I know that you're wealthy with influence. You might not realize it yet, but the deeper you grow in your faith and the more you rely on God's strength...the greater influence you'll have in the lives of others.

Don't hold back from sharing or expressing your faith. You've been blessed with abundance. Give to the poor in spirit. Give to those who need God. Spread the wealth.

My personal influence wouldn't be much...but my influence through my faith and understanding of you is significant. You change lives, God. I know this deeply from my own experience. May I not hold back my wealth of belief from those who are hungry.

Laughter

Do you get enough laughter in your life? What brings you to giggles? What—are you too mature for that? Are you too poised or proper? Taste God's delight in life. He wants you to experience the depths of meaning and ministry, but he also calls you to savor the gift of your time with others and your time walking with him on this earth.

Turn up the joy in your day. Consider adding more music, a comedy movie, stories that celebrate life, and moments when you have absolutely nothing planned except to ponder something funny. Lift up an offering of a joyful heart.

I'll approach today with a cranked-up level of joy. I want to be free of whatever holds me back from extending smiles and helpful gestures. Open my eyes to the joy that's all around me.

Having It All

The debate about whether women can have it all will always be hot. Each of us holds on to versions of what our "all" looks like. The hard truth is that there are always choices and sacrifices to be made. The sweet truth is that when we choose to have faith in the sacrifice that Christ made, we do have it all.

Spiritual abundance isn't something we earn, plan for, coordinate, or schedule in our lives. It's a gift. And it's all yours.

I had a warped version of "having it all" until I came to you with nothing but my broken heart, my sin, and my hunger. Everything looks different now. There isn't a level to achieve, there's a God to adore. This truly is having it all.

Plenty

The cornucopia was a symbol of food and abundance in the fifth century B.C. Yet most of us only learned about it in grade school at Thanksgiving. As a fifth grader, my version of food abundance would've been a stash of Junior Mints! But, we heard that abundance was a cornucopia, a horn-shaped woven basket overflowing with fruits and vegetables.

Do you question whether there's abundance in your life? Do you ask God for sweets when he's provided you with a bounty of vegetables? Consider what you're longing for, and compare it to God's best for you. There's a good chance you're standing in the land of plenty right now. Accept the offering of your good life…and remember to give thanks.

I have more than I need. I have more than I'm able to keep track of. May I only have desires for whatever you want me to take hold of, God. Thank you for this bountiful life.

Toss a Title

Women! We have such simple goals—we want to be healers, givers, mothers, wives, best friends, contributors, leaders, mediators, protectors, shepherds, moderators, controllers, caregivers, helpmates, teachers, servants, designers, contractors...did I leave any of your favorites off the list?

Some roles are assigned to us (without our even realizing it), others we step into eagerly, and still more we take on because we're trying to become something we aren't. Review your list of job titles; ask God which ones are intended for you. Delegate or toss the rest. Living the abundant life sometimes requires that we get rid of a few things first.

Am I wearing a hat that doesn't even belong to me? I tend to take over things before I ask you if they fit into my purpose. It's time to delegate, relinquish control, and give more of myself to the roles you choose for me.

Love's Mark

What marks your speech, your walk, your interaction with strangers, your work, your patience with family? Observe yourself for a day, a week, or longer. See if there's proof of your faith and your personal journey with God. Are you inclined toward joy, compassion, conscientiousness, kindness, and authenticity? Or do you bury these evidences of belief beneath your scars of the past and symbols of worldly success?

God's love leaves an impression in the material of your soul. Let this be the mark of your identity and value.

Is there proof of your hand on my life? Do I speak and act differently because I know and love the God of sea and sky? May my life be marked by my love for you.

Made for More

I sometimes catch myself stopping short of giving my all. I know when I'm living only a portion of the life God intends for me, because I feel that burden of loss and dissatisfaction. My pride and my worry and my track record all rise up to create a barrier between where I stop and the far-reaching life God is guiding me toward.

When you call out to God because you crave more meaning and significance, he'll ask you to examine your heart and your actions. What barriers separate you from a faith of substance? Make the choice to give your all so that you can receive *his* all for your life.

When I hold back, please nudge me forward so that I'll express who I am and what I'm feeling. I've missed too many opportunities because I was scared and reluctant to trust you. Free me from this worry.

Second Helpings

It's hard to refuse second helpings. The next spoonful is as tantalizing as the first. We don't want to refuse the continuation of pleasure, even if the second helpings add up to undesired love handles. Just as your mind overrides your physical fullness and says yes to that next slice of cake, your spirit can override your mind.

When you surrender to what is best for your life, you can appreciate the blessing of the first serving without having to indulge in the next offering. You can savor what you have rather than mourning what you don't. Replace misleading hungers with second helpings of contentment and peace of mind.

It all looks so good. I do want more than I can handle, more than any one person should have, and certainly more than I need. Help me learn to hunger only for what is of you.

Goldilocks

Do you try out people, jobs, dreams, and even your faith to see if it suits your fancy? We've learned to evaluate all of our choices. That's responsible, right? But this overdeveloped desire to get the perfect deal, relationship, or path of faith can keep you from experiencing the joy of everyday moments. Real living and real faith happen in the trenches, not just on the mountaintop.

I believe that sometimes God is merely asking us to commit to where we're at, so that he can work on us. And so he can show us how he turns ordinary living into extraordinary living. Commit your days to God, and commit to stepping into your life with hope.

*Why is it so hard to stand firm in my life as it is?
While I grab on to one thing, I'm always looking
past it to see what else might come my way. Help
me focus on the work you're doing in me and in my
life right now. Don't let me throw that away.*

A Woman's Strength

It takes a lot of emotional strength to be a woman. The pressures can be great. We press on through pain, through adversity, through change, through times when life isn't all we had hoped for *and* when life is more than we'd hoped and we're struggling to keep up!

Your true strength is discovered when you rely on God's vision and love. Even if—especially if—you've never been able to rely on anyone, give yourself over to the abundance of God's care. You won't believe how good it feels to be wrapped in endless support.

Support groups are great, but they have nothing on you, God. I can come to you at any time and for any help I need. I'm slow to ask for help, but I'm getting better at it. Embrace me. I want to feel the protection and strength of my Savior.

Contentment

Words of Contentment

On that day they offered great sacrifices, rejoicing
because God had given them great joy. The
women and children also rejoiced. The sound of
rejoicing in Jerusalem could be heard far away.

Nehemiah 12:43

If they obey and serve him,
they will spend the rest of their days in prosperity
and their years in contentment.

Job 36:11

The precepts of the Lord are right,
giving joy to the heart.
The commands of the Lord are radiant,
giving light to the eyes.

Psalm 19:8

Show me your ways, O Lord,
teach me your paths;
guide me in your truth and teach me,
for you are God my Savior,
and my hope is in you all day long.

Psalm 25:4-5

Satisfy us in the morning with your unfailing love,
that we may sing for joy and be glad all our days.

PSALM 90:14

⁓

A man can do nothing better than to eat
and drink and find satisfaction in his work.
This too, I see, is from the hand of God, for
without him, who can eat or find enjoyment?

ECCLESIASTES 2:24-25

⁓

I know what it is to be in need, and I know
what it is to have plenty. I have learned the
secret of being content in any and every
situation, whether well fed or hungry, whether
living in plenty or in want. I can do everything
through him who gives me strength.

PHILIPPIANS 4:12-13

⁓

Godliness with contentment is great gain. For
we brought nothing into the world, and we
can take nothing out of it. But if we have food
and clothing, we will be content with that.

1 TIMOTHY 6:6-8

Rise Up or Settle Down

What were you doing when you were told to settle down as a child? Clapping during a hymn at church? Playing spoons at the restaurant? Savoring candy (loudly) at a sibling's recital? As an adult, now you get to decide whether you want to settle down. I don't mean the "get married, have kids" settling down, I mean the "act a certain way" mandate.

Don't edit out the moments of happiness and creativity. When you feel the urge to laugh or the inclination to sing along to a favorite song, let it out! Give your spirit of joy a chance to express itself!

I want to express myself and my happiness. Why do I always temper my joy with a dose of maturity and proper behavior? I've held back from delighting in your wonder for too long. I'll let the joy you give me rise up as I sing praises to you and to this life.

Wellspring

When joy rises to the surface of your emotions, do you let it change your mood, your experience, your sense of possibility? Or do you hold it back for some reason? Maybe you've been hurt when you let your guard down? Or maybe there are so many concerns and trials to consider that joy seems an improper use of time and energy and self.

Real happiness, pure joy, is never a waste. And it can never be used up. God's heart is our wellspring of joy. When a wave of delight comes over you, let it sweep you into his presence. Let the curious wonder of joy draw you to a life rich with blessings.

I'm relatively happy. But I've noticed that this happiness doesn't necessarily impact my daily perspective as it should. Why doesn't it influence the way I treat others and the way I respond to your leading? I'm not going to hold back anymore.

Sliding Toward Yes

Do you recognize this loop of thought: *I don't think so. That probably won't work. I'd rather not. What if something bad happens? Why bother at all? Not this time. No. Absolutely not.* Ah, the slippery slope of no. It begins with doubt and slides on into full negativity. Have you been on this ride?

Consider taking a similar ride, but one that is redirected by faith's possibility: *I might. That could work. I'll think about it. This could really work. Why not? This timing is perfect. Yes. Absolutely!*

Stop me when my thoughts start to spiral downward.
I have your sweet mercy and endless grace, and yet
I dwell on the negative blips or my projected fears
during the day. Help me to set my mind on things
from above so that my spirit and mood soar.

First Impression

Days when I wake up motivated and ready for my tasks are good days. A sense of anticipation comes over me, and I feel…happy. Glad. Hopeful. But other mornings I wake up with a slight tremor of dread or restlessness. There might be a huge deadline or an uncomfortable conversation slated for the day. Or I just feel "off."

Too often we let our first impression—our wake-up mood—dictate the rest of the day. Contentment comes when we give over those initial bits of dread, fear, reluctance, or even laziness to God. Consider it a morning offering. Release these to God so he can shape them into something useful. Turn first impressions into expressions of faith.

I think I'll be giving my first impressions to you a lot in the near future. I need a retraining of my heart and mind. Let my first thoughts be of thankfulness and my first words be of praise to you.

Mimic God's Words

Conversations with others can lift your spirit. But your inner dialogue can go downhill when you meet with negative people. It's vital to spiritually prepare yourself for these conversations. Before you start to mimic the neighbor, friend, or coworker who laments every turn of life, focus on words of God to turn your heart upward.

Consider Philippians 4:8: "Finally, brothers, whatever is true, whatever is noble, whatever is right, whatever is pure, whatever is lovely, whatever is admirable—if anything is excellent or praiseworthy—think about such things." And speak of such things!

My own routine...my monologue...has become very worldly and even negative. How did the words I focus on become these words of destruction? I will release those and turn to the words of Philippians—words that give life and faith.

Come On, Get Happy

Did you grow up in a home that was nurturing, joyful, and creative? Or did you have to figure out a way to happiness on your own? Some of us take a long time to experience happiness. The certainty of God's unconditional love provides us with a current of contentment. But happiness requires a nudge now and then.

I nudge by listening to music or buying fresh pads of sketch paper and new pens. Maybe you finger-paint. Bake and decorate cookies. Build a sandcastle. Plan a trip. Read a romance novel. Get goofy with your child. Eat an entire coconut cream pie. Simple pleasures cultivate a heart of happiness!

Joy to the world! You came to save us all. The world is beyond beautiful. I can't stop staring at the moon. And I love the taste of a good nectarine. Oh, Lord...remind me to celebrate all these blessings.

On Your Way

Where are you off to? You look so busy. Can I say it? You even look a bit harried. I get that way sometimes. Have you ever caught yourself holding your breath for long stretches of time? I've done that! No wonder we get anxious or suddenly lose steam and all sense of direction.

Did you just step over this moment to get to the next one? What's your hurry? There will never be another today like today. Give yourself time to breathe. While you're on your way to great things, you might be missing the greatest thing of all—your life!

I've hurdled more than a few moments to think ahead about my job or my agenda. I feel compelled to because life and family become overwhelming. God, turn my attention to the present so that I can honor each day you give me.

Savoring Satisfaction

When is enough really enough? Are you satisfied with your purchase of a great skirt...or do you immediately want to buy two more just like it in different colors? Have you moved into a bigger home and then wished for something with more amenities? Did you take your dream vacation that wasn't nearly as good as you imagined it?

You'll miss out on a lot of living if you're never satisfied. The power of "want" always overrides the truth and beauty of your experience. Practice the art of satisfaction. Start building up your daily life by embracing it, seeing the good, and celebrating each gift of goodness that comes your way.

My wants sneak up on me, God. I'll barely think of them, and then an opportunity to satisfy them arises and I'm obsessed. Mostly I want material luxuries, not necessities. Give me a pure heart that longs for wholeness, not the emptiness of wanting.

Look Carefully

Examine your life as it is, not as you want it to be or as someone else tells you it should be. Contentment comes when we face the day before us without pretense or lies and own up to who we are. There are so many ways to shape today and to turn toward goodness, delight, and purpose.

Your decisions will be wiser, your hope brighter, and your steps more sure when you remove the rose-colored glasses and see the brilliant colors of a real life—the life God has for you. Look closely; it's breathtaking.

This is a kaleidoscope life you have given me. I don't want to settle for a fake image of what life is about. I want it all...the brilliant colors of sadness, hope, uncertainty, and peace. My contentment becomes brighter the more I rest with your faithfulness.

The Contents of a Life

What fills your life? Do you gather friends together often? Do your children make you smile and fuel your purpose? Does work reward with feelings of accomplishment and perseverance? Does your commitment to exercise leave you energetic and happy?

A life of contentment comes from the good, lovely, substantial contents of your life. Are the things you believe in evident through your actions, words, and choices? Gather in your heart all the hope, compassion, integrity, faith, and kindness it can hold—these are the roots of your contentment.

I don't always fill up with things and thoughts that are pleasing to you. I can go the way of selfish or fearful too often. I want the contents of my heart to be the hope of your love and the endless supply of peace you give to those who come to you.

Intentional Living

Words of Intentional Living

In your unfailing love you will lead
the people you have redeemed.

EXODUS 15:13

Walk in all the way that the LORD your
God has commanded you, so that you
may live and prosper and prolong your
days in the land that you will possess.

DEUTERONOMY 5:33

May the words of my mouth and the meditation
of my heart be pleasing in your sight,
O LORD, my Rock and my Redeemer.

PSALM 19:14

You will become wise,
and your knowledge will give you pleasure.
Your insight and understanding will protect you
and prevent you from doing the wrong thing.

PROVERBS 2:10-12 TEV

Whenever you possibly can,
do good to those who need it. Never tell your
neighbors to wait until tomorrow
if you can help him now.

PROVERBS 3:27-28 TEV

~~~~~

Whatever your hand finds to do, do it with
all your might, for in the grave, where you
are going, there is neither working nor
planning nor knowledge nor wisdom.

ECCLESIASTES 9:10

~~~~~

No good tree bears bad fruit, nor does
a bad tree bear good fruit. Each tree
is recognized by its own fruit.

LUKE 6:43-44

~~~~~

Always give yourselves fully to the work
of the Lord, because you know that your
labor in the Lord is not in vain.

1 CORINTHIANS 15:58

Drawing Straws

Let's see, which to choose. They all look about the same. If you choose the long one, you'll surely get what you want out of the situation. If you are sadly a bad guesser and select the stubby one, you're destined to fall short of your goals. You're doomed. No pressure, now choose.

Okay, you probably don't draw straws to decide whom to marry, which job to take, or where to invest your money. Yet, is your system any more spiritually valid? Do you pray over concerns? Do you take your pending decisions to God's Word? Don't leave your life up to chance—give it over to God; he'll draw you closer to his wisdom.

I've gambled away too many choices because I approached them without your wisdom. No more. I want you to know exactly what is going on in my life, and I want to base my decisions on the certainty of your leading. I won't leave the state of my faith to chance.

Willing and Able

Can't. Won't. Which is your word of choice when concocting a reason to not do something? I use them both interchangeably and incorrectly myself. There are likely some very appropriate times to use either word. But *can't* often means you're afraid to try. *Won't* frequently implies fear, pride, or stubbornness.

When you select either word as your "get out of jail free" card, you could be missing out on opportunities to grow, rely on God, discover your gifting, trust others, become more fulfilled, and thrive. That's a lot to give up. A life without excuses becomes a life of purpose. Are you willing?

*God, reveal to me why I hesitate so often to
follow through. I know there is much fear
in me, but why haven't I given my repeat
worries to you? My grip on them is fierce. I
need your strength to let go of my excuses.*

Alive in the World

There's a difference between living and being alive! When you're just living, you ask God to help you survive the day or to have enough energy to appear put together. When you're alive, you feel it to your core. You awaken to God's leading in your heart and soul and through the desires, pursuits, and longings he is giving to you.

When you're alive, you're present for what God is doing in your life and through your life. You clearly hear his whisper of encouragement, and you respond with a "yes, I'll follow!"

When will I understand how truly precious it is to be alive? I have meaningful moments with my family that remind me, but then forget when I'm shopping, driving, talking, planning, or complaining. Show me what being alive in you is all about.

Divine Awareness

Have you ever reached a Saturday and wondered how you got there? What happened to Tuesday? Did that project get done on Wednesday? When life becomes a blur, make a commitment to slow down. (I'd recommend stopping, but you'd probably ignore me.) Pray for God's perspective for your day. Assign value to each and every moment.

We think time flies, but really we're flying through time, propelled by our false sense of urgency. Are worries about next week's meeting crowding out your prayer time? Is your five-year plan more important than the conversation you're having with a friend in need right now? Deliberate living gives you divine awareness.

Give my life focus, Lord. When I set my gaze upon you and your purpose for me, I can see the steps before me. I can clearly distinguish what is of you from what is of the world or my personal desires. Help me be deliberate in all I do.

Knockin'

When opportunity knocks, and before you respond and move forward, check your motives to be sure they are right and pure. Is this possibility about self-gain or true purpose? Does it follow God's leading in your life? Does it fit with the other decisions you have already made with prayerful consideration?

Seek God's wisdom and direction, and ask whether you're being led by a pure heart. "Knock and the door will be opened to you. For everyone who asks receives; he who seeks finds; and to him who knocks, the door will be opened" (Matthew 7:7-8). Before you respond to the latest opportunity, do some knocking of your own.

*Are you leading me today, God? I've felt a pull
for some time now in a certain direction, but I
want to be sure it is from you. I seek your wisdom
and then your peace so that I can know this is the
way to go. Thank you for always answering.*

Instant Messaging God

During the day, we send up little messages to God. Some are mutterings. Some are quick calls for patience, compassion, perspective. Some are general "Lord, help me" cries. While these one-sided conversations don't make for a deep exchange with God, they can lead like stepping stones to a greater prayer life.

Your spontaneous petitions and praises reflect a dependence on God that will lead to a more personal, intimate relationship with him. Follow them to times of focused dialogue with the Creator...after all, this two-sided conversation is life-changing!

I talk a lot at you, God, but I don't always pay attention to your response. Forgive me for the times when all I can do is blurt out my needs and problems. I pray to have my random petitions become a real dialogue with you. Do you have a minute? I want to really talk.

Leave Them Behind

At first, expectations can seem like motivation. The sheer force of their existence can drive you forward in your career, personal goals, relationships, and dreams. But if you rely on expectations for fuel, you'll eventually be disappointed. They offer only the illusion of power and strength.

When you stop living to fulfill expectations and start living to be filled by God's promises, you'll experience the difference. Where there was guilt, you'll have grace. Where there was pressure, you'll have faith. Where there was a shove to succeed, there will be a leading toward purpose.

So many people lay claim to my time and my efforts.
These expectations define my life more than my faith
at times. I want to be discerning so that I'm following
your leading rather than running from pressures.

Resisting Rest

I'm so stubborn, it's amazing I became a person of faith. I am reluctant to ask for help. A friend knew I was going to move a big piece of furniture, and she said, "Please tell me you'll get someone to help you." I smiled and promptly went home and moved it myself. It took a long time, I was sore the next two days, but I did it.

Do you wear your independence like a badge of honor? Do you resist resting in God's strength, the help of another, or even the compassion of friends? Don't go it alone. That burden you're staring at, sizing up, and plotting against on your own is meant to be shared. And you know exactly who to ask for help.

*I need your help. There, I said it. I'm very independent.
You know that about me. But you also see the
ridiculous things I try to do all by myself. It isn't a sign
of strength to resist your peace and your help. Forgive
me for trying to be my own provider and savior.*

Sound Tracks

I settled into my favorite chair with my favorite beverage at my favorite coffee shop—ready for an enjoyable round of reading. But for some reason I had no focus. Then I noticed the frenzied, classical music playing overhead. The music's spiraling intensity undermined my best intentions to concentrate.

What is the distracting or destructive background noise in your life? The relentless criticism of a parent, a boss, or your own mind? The loud rattle of past mistakes trailing behind you? The grating of someone else's negativity? Tune in to God's voice and his calling. It's the intended sound track for your life. It drowns out the chaos and leads you with a rhythm that soothes the soul.

I tune in to words that do not uplift me. I let my heart's beating match the rhythm of the world. Change my sound track, Lord. I want to start humming to your hope and tapping my toes to your timing. You're my new song, and I will sing it boldly.

Tithing Time

Pie charts make for great business presentations. Each segment of the circle represents a portion of the total element being measured—income, population, whatever. In an instant, the presenter can make her point with a visual representation of often intangible elements. If you generated a "my distribution of time" chart, what would your portion spent with God or *for* God look like?

If you're eating humble pie about now, start increasing the size of that slice of your pie chart destined for prayer and devotion. Go from a sliver to a wedge. Redistribute the intangible of time so time for God becomes a significant part of your day.

I'd like to say that everything I do and experience is done with you and for you, God. But that wouldn't be close to true. I have good intentions, but my pure offerings to you are a slim slice of my days. I will work to increase this portion, Lord.

Dreams and Aspirations

Words of Aspiration

Commit your way to the LORD; trust in
him and he will do this: He will make your
righteousness shine like the dawn, the justice
of your cause like the noonday sun.

PSALM 37:5-6

The LORD will fulfill [his purpose] for me;
your love, O LORD, endures forever—
do not abandon the works of your hands.

PSALM 138:8

A longing fulfilled is sweet to the soul.

PROVERBS 13:19

There is surely a future hope for you,
and your hope will not be cut off.

PROVERBS 23:18

Just as honey from the comb is sweet
on your tongue, you may be sure that
wisdom is good for the soul. Get wisdom
and you have a bright future.

PROVERBS 24:13-14 TEV

I alone know the plans I have for you, plans
to bring you prosperity and not disaster,
plans to bring about the future you hope
for. Then you will call to me. You will come
and pray to me, and I will answer you. You
will seek me, and you will find me because
you will seek me with all your heart.

JEREMIAH 29:11-13 TEV

Just as you excel in everything—in faith,
in speech, in knowledge, in complete
earnestness and in your love for us—see
that you also excel in this grace of giving.

2 CORINTHIANS 8:7

Let us hold unswervingly to the hope we
profess, for he who promised is faithful.
And let us consider how we may spur one
another on toward love and good deeds.

HEBREWS 10:23-24

Birthing Plan

The moment a new idea, a dream, or a brilliant goal is conceived is a wonderful thing. You get chills of anticipation. Your imagination leaps to how great life will be when this dream is fulfilled. But then days later, the thrill fades. By the next month you've almost forgotten the lovely goal.

If you want to give birth to a dream, you need a birthing plan! Ask God for the next step. Seek his validation and the support of others. Figure out which of your gifts will have to be honed. Pray each step of the way, and be open to the answers. You never know when God's plan will lead you toward an even bigger dream than the one you conceived.

Help me give birth to this dream, God. What is my next move? Hold me back when I'm supposed to wait. Give me discernment so that I can see where you are leading me. Help me to let go of any dream that is solely of my own making.

Life in 360

I don't always glean what I'm supposed to learn from life situations. My eyes are on the prize of finishing. I'm determined to meet deadlines. I'm motivated by pressure. I'm driven to finish project A so I can move on to project B. Only lately am I realizing how limited my vision of life is.

It's good to have focus. To finish what you start—as long as you don't hurry forth with blinders on. There's so much life happening around you. There are people in need. Doors open for you to walk through. And there's inspiration when you look to the left or the right of the horizon's center. Life in 360 degrees has a beautiful view.

Expand my view, God. I want to take all of life in. When my focus is on my stuff, I miss out on seeing the people in my life, the joy, and the path you present. It will be a lot for me to take in—this new view—but I'm excited.

I Always Thought...

When you gather with friends and the conversation stalls on the mundane activities like laundry, deadlines, carpooling, do you ever stare off into the distance and say, "I always thought life would be different"? When left to your own thoughts, do you dwell on the pursuit that never went anywhere? The idea that never took flight? The relationship that never evolved beyond friendship?

If you give what hasn't happened more importance than what *is* happening, you'll miss the dream God's planting today. And you won't notice the ones he's already fulfilled!

Sometimes I get trapped in the ordinary. I don't want to be a "what if" woman. I want to notice all that you're doing and have done. With this awareness, I can walk with conviction and fearlessness.

Dream a Little Dream

Are you so caught up in today's pressures that you forget to give attention to your hopes? Your dreams? I know. We're all so very practical. There's so much to do today that it's difficult to invest in those dreams. But believe me, they need a bit of your attention. Keep your dreams alive with prayer, time spent reflecting on your goals, and also time spent journaling or pondering the possibilities of your life.

God gives you longings and hopes. Don't let agendas, pressures, and expectations drown out those seeds of your purpose and direction. Dream a little dream.

A little space would do me wonders. I need space in my life, my schedule, and my thought life so that I can think on and pray over all the dreams you give me. You inspire me daily and give me great hope for a future.

Pursuits of a Life

Investment of self, time, money, and ability can meld together and become the launching pad for the life God has for you. Where do you invest your self, money, and ability right now? Do you seek opportunities that are of God? That feel like your calling? That feed your soul? That seem tied to purpose?

The pursuits of your life do matter. They reflect your priorities. They're born of your heart, and they reveal your calling. Redirect your steps today if they do not lead to God's purpose. Take in the wonders and delights that the Creator has orchestrated on your behalf. Celebrate with each step.

Step one. Step two. Step three. These are all mapped out by you and for me. It's incredible. I want to sit with this amazing truth. This time I'm making room for the wonder of it all.

Creator in Action

Inspiration is always such a sweet surprise. Do you get that rush of creativity, thoughts with power and ingenuity behind them, or the pull toward something fresh and wonderful? These great, and somewhat rare, experiences let us peek into the Creator's workshop. We get a glimpse of how God lovingly and joyfully forms miracles.

Give the work of your life over to the Master. He'll blow away the dust, he'll rub out the rough spots, he'll treat it like a brilliant treasure. He'll model the profound love he has for the heart he shaped in you.

My inspiration comes from you. When I feel the incredible joy of an idea coming on, I know it's a gift from your heart to mine. I want to offer it back to you so that you can shape it, smooth it, and refine it into something worthy.

Give Yourself Up

Each of us has a unique voice, gifting, and perspective to contribute. You admire strength and ability in your neighbor, your friend, or your child—but do you recognize such worth in yourself? God does. He sees your very core. His vision encompasses not just what you've done, but all that you're made to accomplish through him.

Don't hold back from contributing who you are and what you have to give. It's too great of a loss for the world to bear. Release your inclination to align your identity with your mistakes, and behold your beauty and value as a new creation in God's grace.

Why do I sell myself short when you have created me, held me close, and breathed life into my spirit? You call me to be a servant, but you don't tell me that what I have to offer is less than that of another. Teach me the balance, Lord. I know I have a lot to give.

Crystal Ball

We might not seek advice from a crystal sphere or from staring at the stars, but we occasionally, foolishly look to things other than God for a vision of what's to come. The amazing part of being a woman of belief is that we know what the future holds. We don't have specific images, numbers, figures, and details, but we have direction and promises.

When you need a glimpse of somewhere to place your hope, look to God. He'll show you exactly what today, tomorrow, and forever holds for you, his child.

What will happen? What will my life be like?
Will my children be well and good? What changes
will take place soon? As much as I want to know
all of this…all that I need to know is that I can
always turn to you, and you will never leave me.

See Yourself

When you look at your family and friends, do you see their gifts so clearly? It's easy to encourage them because their talents shine and their strengths are so evident; meanwhile you are reluctant to accept a compliment. Are you willing to cast yourself in a good light? Do you believe in the purpose and plan God has mapped on your heart?

Today is a chance to claim and honor all that's wonderful in you. Express your gifts. Truly see your intelligence, personality, and uniqueness—they are part of you, and they are evidence of your Maker.

*Lord, what do you see when you look at me? I
see the times I let others down. I see the wounds
that remain open because I refuse to forgive. I see
mistake after mistake. Let me see what you see.
I need to see my life in the light of your love.*

Am I There Yet?

Is this life I'm living really my purpose? Did I miss a turn somewhere? Do you ever scratch your head and wonder such things? Doubts won't destroy dreams, but they certainly can delay them. If you stand before God and play twenty questions, ask for confirmation, direction, and answers.

God doesn't give us hope and then sit back to watch us flounder. He's with us every step of the way; he's leading, he's holding back, and he's carrying us. And when you journey with God—you *are* there, exactly where you're supposed to be.

Sorry for all the questions, but they fill my head, and I have to get them out. Sometimes they lead me astray, away from what you have planned for me. Can my questions be an offering today? May this be my prayer of need, dependence, and trust in your presence.

Hope

Words of Hope

Who cuts a channel for the torrents of rain,
and a path for the thunderstorm,
to water a land where no man lives,
a desert with no one in it,
to satisfy a desolate wasteland and
make it sprout with grass?

JOB 38:25-27

You turned my wailing into dancing; you removed
my sackcloth and clothed me with joy, that my
heart may sing to you and not be silent.
O LORD my God, I will give you thanks forever.

PSALM 30:11-12

Since you are my rock and my fortress,
for the sake of your name lead and guide me.

PSALM 31:3

Teach me to do your will,
for you are my God;
may your good Spirit
lead me on level ground.

PSALM 143:10

You were wearied by all your ways,
but you would not say, "It is hopeless."
You found renewal of your strength,
and so you did not faint.

ISAIAH 57:10

~

Jesus answered, "Those who drink this water will
get thirsty again, but those who drink the water
that I will give them will never be thirsty again.
The water that I will give them will become in
them a spring which will provide them with
life-giving water and give them eternal life."

JOHN 4:13-14 TEV

~

Just as the sufferings of Christ flow over into
our lives, so also through Christ our comfort
overflows. If we are distressed, it is for your
comfort and salvation; if we are comforted, it is
for your comfort, which produces in you patient
endurance of the same sufferings we suffer.

2 CORINTHIANS 1:5-6

Breaking the Ice

Ice fishing. That's not a topic you ponder every day. The extreme cold combined with the need for great patience would send me running for the nearest sunny beach. Yet there's something noble in this sport. The fishermen cut a hole in the desolate surface of nature's terrain and tap into water teeming with life below. It's an act of hope.

Our daily horizon can become an expanse of white noise, cold encounters, and frozen emotions. But if we break the surface of nominal living with prayer and commitment to the things of God, we'll see that our hearts are teeming with life and purpose. It is then that we can cast our line in the waters of hope.

*I have been frozen. Locked into a pattern of activity,
going through my days without prayer and without
considering the deeper purpose of my waking life.
God, help me to break through the surface so that
I reach into my soul to your living waters.*

Tower of Fear

When my fear of a situation or outcome becomes great, I use absolute terms like "all or nothing," "always," and "never." I predict fear-based scenarios: It will be a disaster. Nobody will like me. I'll fail. Others always fail me. This builds and builds. When I come down from my tower of fear, I'm dizzy from the swift shift in altitude.

What escalating worries, anxieties, and doubts build up so quickly that before you know it, you're standing miles above reality on a very weak platform of lies and deceptions? Come down from the tower. Better yet, stay tethered to God's truth, love, and wisdom before you start the climb.

I put up such walls with my absolutes based on fear. God, give me a spirit of peace and humility. Only when I give each fear over to you as it arises will the tower of my insecurities tumble.

Mercy, Mercy Me

Are troubled skies forming? Are dark clouds covering your life? It can be a lonely experience to prepare for a personal storm. Maybe those you depend on most are the ones causing the earth to shake beneath you. Are the wild winds of fear, anxiety, or sorrow gathering inside of you?

When the sky does open up and the first drops fall, there's shelter for you in the arms of God. He will carry you through this. He will protect you from what brews in your heart and what blows across the landscape of life as you know it. There is no trial or trouble, sin or sadness, defeat or depression that will keep you from God's sweet mercy.

I've been through this storm before, but when the winds start, it always sends me trembling. I struggle through the same problems and doubts to get back to faith. Why do I make it so hard? You're right here with me, Lord.

Come So Far

Visit your personal scrapbook. Where have you been, and who were you? What has God done in your life and through your obedience? How did he make something you tried to tear apart into something whole and useful? Are there parts of your life that never made sense until God put the pieces back together in a new way?

Sadly, we often equate mistakes with absolute failure...as though redemption didn't exist. You've come so far—and not as a result of random collisions of right time/right place. Recognize the journey and be grateful for it—God has brought you here.

Only you have brought me here. Only your love has carried me through the trenches of difficulty. Only your mercy has covered me. Only your intervention has saved me. Only your grace has redeemed me.

Light Your Way

The look of the sun rising over a field of wheat is much different than the view of morning's first light over the white slopes of a mountain. Your experience of God's light cast across your life changes with the scenery of your journey.

When the terrain of your day is rough, God's light is a warm glow. When life soars smoothly, there are bright rays of joy. When you're stumbling along the cliffs of trial, his love is a lighthouse's beam, directing you home. No matter what you're experiencing, God's hope radiates across the landscape of your life.

When I'm cast in darkness I need only to look for your light. It's my focal point and my beacon. Lead me home, Lord.

Matter of Convenience

Those 24/7 corner markets are fabulous. I can go there for potato chips during a late night of work. When I want to perk up midafternoon, I can go get a cup of coffee. And on those days when I wake up at dawn, I can walk to the market, get a donut, and have a brief exchange with someone else who is alert at that ridiculous hour.

God's hope is available to us 24 hours a day. Pursue it when you need comfort. Go to it when you need a pick-me-up. Ask for it when you feel alone in the universe. Hope is not elusive or a great mystery. It always exists. And it is available right when you need it.

Sometimes I wander in circles looking for acceptance and connection. Your embrace is open to take me in, reassure me, and lead me toward your purpose for my life. My aimlessness turns toward direction and hope.

Open to Love

Lost love and broken promises can sever our ability to hope for the best. We might say we want to heal, yet most of us describe the times we've been hurt with sadness or anger that is fresh, raw, and very close to the surface. Are you nurturing your pain more than your hope?

When you give your wounds to God's healing mercy, he'll expand your heart to make room for hope, faith, and new experiences. He'll restore your openness to love.

I've been nursing these long-endured emotional injuries with all the wrong remedies. I want to experience complete restoration. Please separate me from my pain. You remind me that I'm your child. I don't want my wounds to be my identity ever again.

His Embrace

As much as we might wish for it, our everyday faith doesn't always have the intimacy of a one-on-one chat with God in our living rooms. There are times when God seems far away. He isn't absent…nevertheless, when that sense of distance rises up, it can throw us for a loop. It can send some on a journey of struggle.

If you're facing a time of distance or silence, rest in the knowledge of God's presence. Stand on the security of his faithfulness. Start a conversation with God, like you would with a best friend, and allow the dialogue to unfold. God is there. Your hope will remind you of his everpresent embrace.

When there is silence, Lord, help me to seek the solace of your Word and of your peace. These, too, are here to guide me and bring me comfort and show me the workings of faith—even during troubled times. May my earnest prayers reach you always.

Life Adjustment

The world's version of hope might consist of an attitude adjustment, but faith's version of hope adjusts everything. Here are ways you can get hope to take on dimension in daily living: Let it infuse your speech with uplifting, generous, and positive words. Come at your trials and problems from a wide angle that makes room for possibility. Start your day knowing that up ahead there will be good conversations, interactions, decisions, and chances to reach out.

There are many ways for hope to be manifested in your life.

God, I want to be hope filled. Give me your eyes for every situation. Give me your heart for others, my family, and my own life. Refresh my sense of possibility so that I anticipate good things.

Is It Any Wonder?

When in the presence of children, it's fun to play make-believe. You can create a kingdom right in your living room. You can play catch with the moon. You can string stars onto a necklace. You can turn into a dove and soar to heaven.

Hope isn't fantasy, but it holds the same promise as time spent pretending the utterly impossible is completely possible. Hope isn't hiding from real life; it's embracing the realness of God. And about those fruit of the imagination listed above...God can do them all. Is it any wonder he makes belief out of a sprinkle of hope?

Nothing is impossible for you! You aren't a magician; you're the Maker of all I see and know...and all I don't see and don't know. My far-reaching imagination can never surpass the wonders of your real power.

Wholeness

Words of Wholeness

You, O Lord, are always my shield from danger;
you give me victory and restore my courage.

Psalm 3:3 tev

As a father is kind to his children,
so the Lord is kind to those who honor him.
He knows what we are made of;
he remembers that we are dust.

Psalm 103:13-14 tev

I will lead the blind by ways they have not known,
along unfamiliar paths I will guide them;
I will turn the darkness into light before them
and make the rough places smooth.

Isaiah 42:16

[Jesus] said to her, "Daughter, your
faith has healed you. Go in peace."

Luke 8:48

If you have any encouragement from being
united with Christ, if any comfort from his
love, if any fellowship with the Spirit, if any
tenderness and compassion, then make my joy
complete by being like-minded, having the
same love, being one in spirit and purpose.

PHILIPPIANS 2:1-2

No one has ever seen God; but if we love one
another, God lives in us and his love is made
complete in us. We know that we live in him and
he in us, because he has given us of his Spirit.

1 JOHN 4:12-13

The Lamb at the center of the throne
will be their shepherd; he will lead them
to springs of living water. And God will
wipe away every tear from their eyes.

REVELATION 7:17

Remains to Be Seen

I've walked out of a bad movie before. I didn't care whether I saw the ending. But I'm a bit less casual when it comes to my life. I like to know how things will turn out. I like to see whether my efforts to help someone will pay off. I crave closure for past situations. I want distinct endings before I move on. And I long to know what my future holds.

Does it bug you when you only see a speck of the big picture? God calls you to pray, participate, follow, and surrender; he doesn't call you to do his job. When you move forward without seeing the whole picture, God is at work, making you whole.

With uncertainties circling about me and concerns facing my family, I'm not so good with letting go of the outcome. I pray for your will, and then I try to take back control. God, I want to rest in your embrace. I will trust you even when I'm scared.

Gusts of Grace

Trials sweep through your life like storm winds. They press you against a wall until you can't breathe. They bury you under burdens too heavy to lift on your own. Have you been thrown by such forces?

The trials that knock you off your feet are not strong enough or powerful enough to destroy the foundation of God's faithfulness. They're nothing compared to the gusts of grace that blow through us and clean out the loss, regret, and disappointment. Wait for his restoration. He will rebuild your life with the secure materials of grace and hope.

I'm still surprised I got out from under recent burdens. It was all your doing, Lord. I give you the credit and the praise. The struggle was so great, I couldn't move. You released me and gave me more strength and understanding to move forward into good things.

All Good

Unknowingly, we carry many wounds with us from the past into the present. We juggle shadows of them while trying to accomplish something new in our lives. We're so desperate to move on from trials that we neglect to glean the knowledge and understanding of God's faithfulness that comes from living our tough circumstances. So the pain stays with us.

Goodness can bloom from the hurtful experiences you've tried to forget. Those wounds helped shape who you are. Those wounds are part of the story of God's mercy. They're part of your journey from broken to whole.

I present a good front to others, but on the inside, a strong sense of failure burns. Help me to sit with the past rough parts of my journey. Help me to learn from them before I let them go. In your hands they become wisdom.

If It Ain't Broke

Most people would espouse the philosophy that it's best not to try to fix something that isn't blatantly broken. This seems like sage advice. We're busy, and we don't have time to waste. But because of this busyness, we often don't recognize when a part of us is broken and in dire need of fixing.

We juggle the needs of our families, we face obstacles with flair, and we keep life moving along. We bury our hurts and our needs under the demands of the day. The world might say to "leave well enough alone," but just getting by is not the same as wholeness. Life is intended to be abundant. Bring your brokenness to the Lord.

Time to be fixed. Time to admit I'm not perfect and that I'm not whole. I'm functional, and there's a big difference. Expose the broken places that I have skillfully patched up with human Band-Aid solutions. Grant me healing, God, from the inside out.

Between Engagements

Obligations. Responsibilities. Commitments. Events. Appointments. Has your personality taken on the characteristics of an overachiever, a chronic doer, a party planner? When activities shove aside active listening, praying, and meditating, you're usually left without energy, direction, or joy.

Give yourself room to think. Make time between engagements to engage in devotional living. If you rely on God to show up for everything you've penned into your week's schedule, isn't it time to show up for your Creator? No agenda in hand. No deadlines. Come to give and to be filled.

Lead me to the sanctuary of a quiet spirit. I haven't had that in a long time. I start out looking for peace but usually wind up volunteering for some task instead. I've depleted my reserves. Oh, how I long to be filled by your love, Lord.

Clank!

When I walk over to the long line of carts at the local wholesale store, I—without fail—select the cart with the loudest squeak and wobbliest wheel. Every time! It seems like too much effort to return it outside and select another...so I push on, pretending I don't hear the obnoxious, earsplitting clatter of my metal chariot.

We often maneuver through the tight turns of life with our broken parts and our human instability clanging away. All the while pretending we don't notice. All the while wishing we had exchanged our faults for forgiveness early on. Somehow we think it's noble to drag our loud problems with us rather than ask God to tend to them. We're so mistaken!

Oops. How loud are my problems? They certainly do clamor in my head and heart. God, give me the silence of well-being. Direct me toward measures of healing that soothe my spirit and seal my wounds for eternity.

Finding Yourself

The sculptor's hand can only break the spell,
To free the figures slumbering in the stone.

MICHELANGELO

When Michelangelo looked at a particular mass of stone, he saw his statue within. If we look at the mass of our ego, wants, needs, hurts, healings, faults, and strengths, can we see the "us" God created within? We must let God chip away those pieces that no longer belong in our lives (some never did belong). We must sculpt out our purpose with the chisel of faith and let our sins, heartaches, lies, and selfish desires tumble to the ground. Our way to wholeness begins with letting go.

I pray that I haven't disappointed you like I've disappointed myself. Lord, don't give up on me. Bless me with times of letting go so that the real me emerges complete and beautiful under the Creator's gaze.

Mine...Yours...God's

As a young girl, I read a story about two sisters who, after a fight, stretched a jump rope across the middle of their shared bedroom floor—each claimed sole occupancy of a half. Well, soon they both needed what was on the other's side, including the closet for clothes and the door to exit!

When we become judgmental, jealous, or self-righteous, we draw lines down the middle of our homes, churches, places of work, and neighborhoods. But we need others in order to live a whole life. Jesus tells us to "Love your neighbor" not because it's good PR for God, but because it's the way to wholeness, unity, and the expression of his heart.

Where are my dividing lines, God? I've lost track.
My envy or anger has established unnecessary
boundaries and limits in my life. Some relationships
have been repaired, but others remain in pieces.
Please heal my heart so that I will seek wholeness.

A Place to Belong

When visiting a small town, all it takes is one stop at the local market or the coffee shop and you're up on the news about colorful residents and the latest marriage and birth celebrations. In no time you can feel less of an outsider and more like a regular.

We all understand the desire to connect. God designed us to want to belong. For some it is less intense; for others it's motivation to create community wherever they go. Follow your heart when it is ready to connect with others. Step over the fear, insecurity, or obstacles, and trust the longing that leads to wholeness through fellowship.

God, I feel the tug to join in and to be a part of life around me, yet I use my family's needs and schedule as an excuse to keep a distance. Lead me to the right people. I want to belong and feel the wholeness of community.

A Whole Life

During each life season we tend to define our existence by a few things: School and work. Work and dating. Work and marriage. Marriage and family. Children and parents. What defines your life right now? Consider expanding the list. Our priorities will take up more of our time and effort, but they should not replace a complete life.

Open up to your spiritual growth, friendships, development of your gifts, service to those outside of your family, commitment to follow through in areas you've short-changed. Talk to God about what your life needs in order to be whole again.

I haven't felt complete in a while. My life seems to be all about family. It's good, yet I feel an ache for friendships and a hunger for faith. God, help me to find a balance so that I can serve my priorities and seek a whole, fulfilling life that pleases you.

Discovery

Words of Discovery

Can you discover the limits and bounds of
the greatness and power of God? The sky
is no limit for God, but it lies beyond your
reach. God knows the world of the dead,
but you do not know it. God's greatness is
broader than the earth, wider than the sea.

JOB 11:7-9 TEV

O God, you are my God, earnestly I seek you;
my soul thirsts for you, my body longs for you,
in a dry and weary land where there is no water.

PSALM 63:1

Beg for knowledge; plead for insight.
Look for it as hard as you would for silver
or some hidden treasure. If you do, you will know
what it means to fear the LORD
and you will succeed in learning about God.
It is the LORD who gives wisdom;
from him come knowledge and understanding.

PROVERBS 2:3-6 TEV

Do not abandon wisdom, and she will protect you; love her, and she will keep you safe. Getting wisdom is the most important thing you can do. Whatever else you get, get insight. Love wisdom, and she will make you great. Embrace her, and she will bring you honor. She will be your crowning glory.

PROVERBS 4:6-9 TEV

~~~

From now on I will tell you of new things, of hidden things unknown to you.

ISAIAH 48:6

~~~

You will call upon me and come and pray to me, and I will listen to you. You will seek me and find me when you seek me with all your heart.

JEREMIAH 29:12-13

~~~

Without faith it is impossible to please God, because anyone who comes to him must believe that he exists and that he rewards those who earnestly seek him.

HEBREWS 11:6

Turning Corners

I love to walk through a city for hours. Unlike suburbs where one uninterrupted main road can run the length of a development or a community, the city offers the gift of blocks. I walk so many strides, and there I am, standing at a new corner. I can turn the corner and encounter a new discovery, adventure, and view.

In your life you'll encounter long, continuous parts of your path. But just when you have the horizon memorized, an intersection in the form of a decision, a revelation, or a change will present itself. God is leading you to turn a new corner in your life! Embrace the discoveries up ahead.

I'm a bit nervous but also excited. I know change is coming, and I welcome it. Only when I embrace the opportunities to rely on you completely will I ever discover the lessons and wonders you want me to gather.

Enjoy the Unexpected

A sense of control is important in a woman's life. People are depending on us! Managing time, family details, and finances is a good thing. But don't let the necessity of organization turn into a need to control everything that comes along—people, conversations, and opportunities.

My quest to control the unexpected has brought with it more sorrow than satisfaction. Can you relate? It can feel so right to take charge, but by doing so, we cut short the blessings God presents. And we miss out on the unexpected delights that come our way!

Tightness in the pit of my stomach is my usual warning that I'm about to lose control of a situation. God, why am I so anxious? I have great faith in you. It would be so nice to enjoy the gifts of unexpected events, people, and possibilities. Free me from myself, Lord.

Leading Lady

In the movie *The Holiday* there's a scene where a main character is lamenting her heartbreak…caused by a louse. The older gentleman dining with her is a retired screenwriter from Hollywood's glamour days; he sums up her problem: she always casts herself as the "friend" when she is meant to be the leading lady!

Become the leading lady of your life. This doesn't mean you upstage others at work. It doesn't mean you are never a friend. It does mean that you stop trying to be someone you aren't, and you step up into the role God has shaped for you. Brilliant.

God, show me what it takes to be the leading lady of my life. I can't wait to walk with confidence, knowing that I'm not pretending but am purposed for this path and part. Give me the courage to step forward as I trust your direction.

Harvest of Honor

You reap what you sow. Don't let the common usage of this faith formula deceive you. It has great significance for your daily life and your future. Are you harvesting good behaviors, relationships, and experiences in each season of your life? If not, what is in your sower's pouch?

If you regularly reap half-truths or unfulfilled promises, examine whether you are planting honesty and faithfulness. Are you up front with yourself, God, and others? Do you follow through? Ask God for the seeds of wisdom, sincerity, and integrity, and offer him a heart prepared to grow goodness.

I want to invest my efforts in goodness. Give me the right seeds to plant at the right time. I will nurture them and lift their harvest up to you. I hope to reap good relationships, kindness, faithfulness, and joy to honor you.

Creation in Motion

You're part of the history of the world and the history of God's people. When you think of your life as insignificant—a blip on the eternity screen—you're forgetting how vital your role is. Each story of faith is remarkable. Each life lived under God's grace is a testimony. Each woman's journey as a person of prayer and purpose is monumental.

God sees you. Your heart, your faults, your gifts, your truth. You are a part of creation in motion. Those who came before and those who come after will never offer God or the world the gift of you. Give it and live it! Start to see what God sees in you!

*My days matter. My prayers matter. My commitment
to faith matters. Show me how to communicate my
testimony. I don't feel like I have enough to say, but
I know you give every person the power of a story.
May my dependence on you be the theme of mine.*

Look for It!

Along the shore there are many discoveries to be made. Some rest on the sand's surface, just waiting to be plucked and carried away by a lucky person. Other ocean prizes lie under the rough surface. They won't be found by the lucky, but by the diligent.

Do you gather those treasures that sit atop the path but never look more carefully for those blessings below the surface of conversation, daily living, and brief encounters? Head out into your life with watchful eyes and an attentive heart, and don't forget your yellow plastic shovel. Go deeper. Be the one to discover the buried gems.

God, give me patience to persevere in my search for life's treasures. I'll watch more carefully. I'll stop and pay attention. I'll keep digging until you tell me to stop.

Connecting

My interactions with others can be filled with small talk or distracted conversation. These half-hearted connections with coworkers, family, friends, and strangers aren't because I don't care; they happen because my head is in the clouds or my heart is buried under the weight of worry—either way, I'm bypassing the significance of relationships.

Honor the value of the people God brings to your path. Focus on what they say with their words and with their silence. When responsibilities and commitments fill your mind, your choice to be present for people will lead you to be present in your life.

I want my connections with others to be sincere.
God, when I start to check out of conversations
or my responsibilities to others, lead me back
to focus. May I honor you by honoring others
and savoring the present moment.

Under the Sun

The author of Ecclesiastes hungered to find the meaning of life. But as he examined wealth, labor, freedom, and decadence, he discovered that life itself was meaningless. "What has been will be again, what has been done will be done again; there is nothing new under the sun" (Ecclesiastes 1:9). How can this fit with the faith journey?

Ecclesiastes illuminates the most important truth you can discover: There's nothing of the world you can pursue that will give your life purpose and significance. Not money. Not success. Not a house. Not a picket fence. Not celebrity. Only the pursuit of God will give your life meaning. Following the way of God is the only journey that matters.

I've felt the emptiness of shallow pursuits and the sadness of meaningless endeavors. Only when I came to your heart did I discover purpose for the rest of my journey. There's nothing under the sun more meaningful than the Maker of the sun and his love.

About the Author

Hope Lyda has worked in publishing for 10 years and is the author of several novels, including *Life, Libby, and the Pursuit of Happiness,* and numerous nonfiction titles such as *One Minute with God* and the popular One-Minute Prayers series. When not writing her own books, Hope helps others in their writing endeavors as an editor.

For more information about Hope and all of her books, stop by and visit her website: *www.hopelyda.com.*

Hope can also be reached at:

Hope Lyda
Harvest House Publishers
990 Owen Loop North
Eugene, OR 97402

or at:

HopeLyda@yahoo.com